South Padre Island and Port Isabel

Restaurants

Pat McGrath Avery

ISBN: 978-1-943267-44-6

Red Engine Press
Pittsburgh, PA

Printed in the United States.

||||||||||||||||||||||||||||||||||||||||||||||||||||||||||||||||||||||||||||||

Introduction

One thing that draws us all together regardless of age, nationality, politics or religion is our love of good food. The South Padre Island and Port Isabel area provides plenty of opportunities for residents and visitors to please the taste buds.

With the Gulf of Mexico to the east and the Mexican border to the south, the restaurants offer the best of the sea and our southern neighbors. Diners will find many variations of familiar menu items, and they will seldom be disappointed.

Tacos may not be the same as visitors will find up north and the shrimp will dwarf what is offered by the land-bound states above us. Once you visit, you may never want to leave.

Our restaurants cater to visitors in all four seasons, and I hope this guide helps you find new places, unique dishes and healthy options to enjoy.

Many of our restaurants offer menu choices for the gluten and lactose intolerant diner, diabetics and those with other health requirements. Be sure to ask your server if you have a special need.

For those who love to fish, many of the area restaurants will prepare your catch, as you like it.

In addition to the restaurants in this guide, many of the national and fast-food chains attract diners. Port Isabel is home to Whataburger, Diary Queen, Pizza Hut, McDonald's in Walmart, Subway, Wingstop and Burger King.

On the island, you will find McDonald's, Whataburger, KFC, Dairy Queen, Wingstop, Pizza Hut, Subway and Denny's. Both the Hilton Garden Inn and LaCopa Inn have a Starbucks.

This is not a complete listing of area restaurants, but I've tried to include the most popular choices. Also, the restaurant business is always a financial risk. Restaurants close and new ones open throughout any given year.

In addition to their websites and/or Facebook pages, most have been reviewed on TripAdvisor and Yelp. I added some of the available information from restaurant websites. The information listed should not be associated with the quality of the restaurant.

I have visited many of the locations but not all. Therefore in order to be fair, I've tried not to let my own personal preferences show.

Several locations are dog-friendly (on their patios). To my knowledge, they include the following. In Port Isabel - Causeway Cafe Port Isabel and Will & Jack's. On the island - Boomerang Billy's, BurgerFi, Clayton's, Gabriella's, Padrerita Grill, Palm Street Pier and The Palms Cafe.

Table of Contents

NOTE: Red headers are for South Padre Island, Blue for Port Isabel.

Bada Bing Bagels

1817 Padre Blvd #3
South Padre Island, TX
956-336-9378

www.badabingbagel.com
Facebook: https://www.facebook.com/pg/BagelsSPI/

Hours:

Mon - Sat 8:00 am - 2:00 pm
Sun - 8:00 am - 1:00 pm

Blackbeards

103 East Saturn Lane
South Padre Island
956-761-4379

http://www.blackbeardsspi.com
Facebook: Blackbeards Restaurant

Hours:
Sun - Thu 11:30 am - 9:00 pm
Fri - Sat 11:30 am - 10:00 pm

Happy Hours
Mon - Fri 4:00 pm - 6:00 pm

Established: 1978

Blackbeards is known for their great sandwiches, steak burgers, famous fried seafood platters, specialty gulf shrimp and fish dishes, as well as cooking up your latest catch. All of their dishes are prepared with the unique culinary influence found nowhere else but along the Gulf of Mexico.

The restaurant started with burgers and beer. Today they serve a full menu and offer a full bar. Check out their daily specials.

Boomerang Billy's Beach Bar & Grill

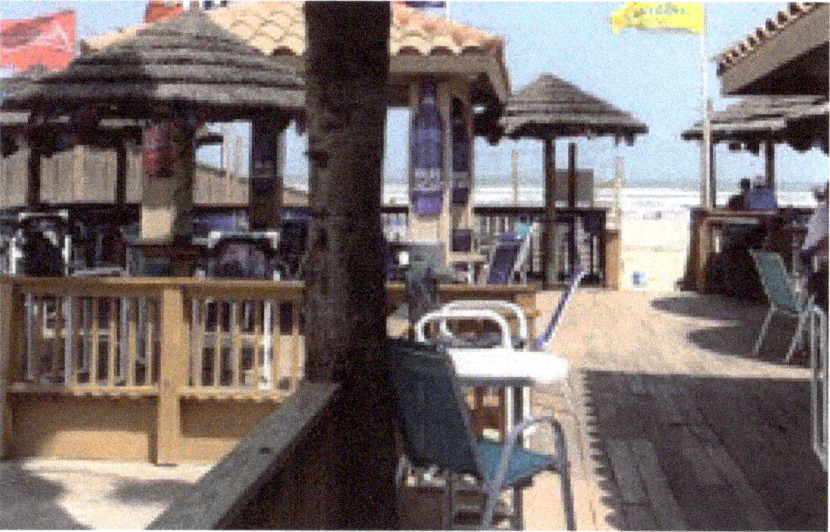

2612 Gulf Blvd
South Padre Island

956-761-2831

www.surfmotelpadre.com
Facebook: Boomerang Billy's Beach Bar & Grill

Hours:
Sunday 12:00pm - 9:00 pm
Monday - Saturday 11:00 am - 9:00 pm

The first and original beach bar on South Padre Island.
Offering live music every weekend.

BurgerFi

5001 Padre Blvd
South Padre Island, TX
956.433.5502

www.burgerfi.com

Owner Donald Kramer takes pride is serving all-natural Angus burgers. BurgerFi offers a wide variety of toppings, hand-cut French fries, craft beers and wine, and natural frozen custards and concretes.

With it modern urban setting, BurgerFi's menu offers specialty items like Kobe beef hot dogs, and focuses on healthy selections. Their beef is grass-fed and contains neither chemicals nor additives.

Cap'n Roy's Seafood Restaurant

1313 Padre Blvd
South Padre Island, TX
956-761-9990

www.capnroys.com
Facebook: Cap'n Roy's

Open everyday at 11:00 am for lunch and dinner
Fresh seafood daily

Causeway Cafe

418 E. Queen Isabella
(Lighthouse Square at the corner of Hwy 100 & Garcia)
Port Isabel, TX
956-433-5004

https://www.mycausewaycafe.com
https://www.facebook.com/causewayportisabel/

The original Causeway Cafe, focusing on fresh, healthy entrees.
All homemade recipes.
Street-side dining and a back garden patio.

Causeway Cafe

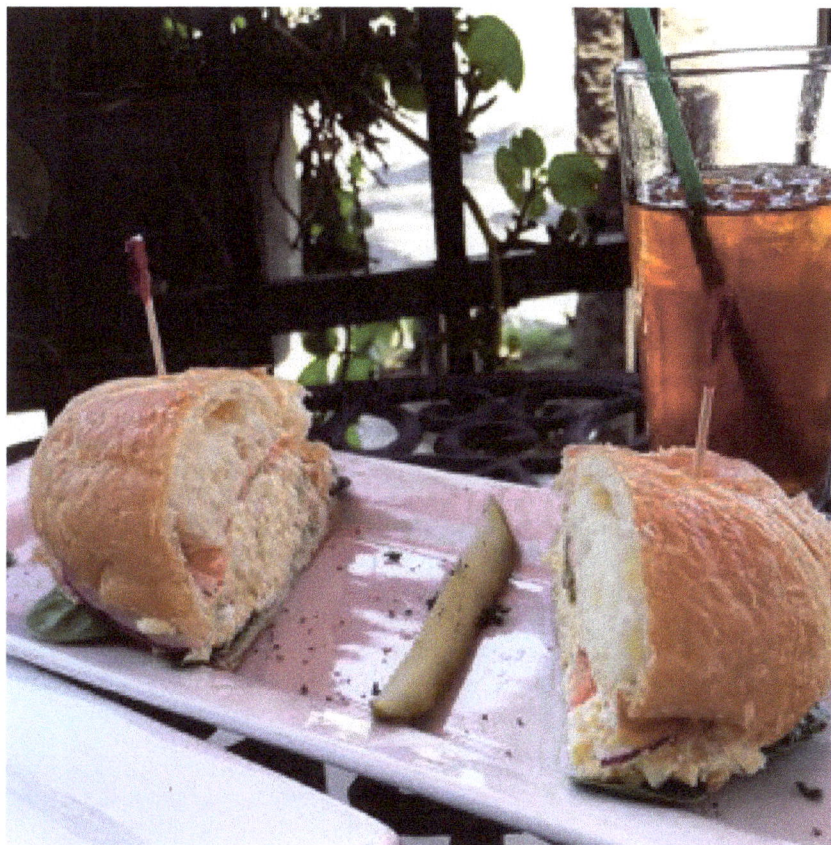

Egg Salad Sandwich and Iced Tea

The Chef House

313 E. Queen Isabella
Port Isabel, TX
956.943.7797

Facebook: The Chef House Restaurant

Hours
Mon Closed
Tue - Fri 8:00 am - 3:00 pm
Sat - Sun 8:00 am - 4:00 pm

Established: 2011

Owners Chef Silvano and Esmeraldo first opened in Port Isabel. They later moved to the island and are now back in Port Isabel at 313 at E. Queen Isabella.

Their use of fresh ingredients and the food presentation are key parts of their success. They offer both a breakfast and lunch, as well as daily specials. All food is prepared fresh for each order. The owners pride themselves on their food and their service.

The Chef House

Enchiladas with tomatillo sauce

Chilitto Pikin Mexican Restaurant

3305 Padre Blvd
South Padre Island, TX
956-433-5484

Facebook: www.facebook.com/Chilitto

Hours
Tue - Sat 11:00 am - 9:00 pm
Sun - Mon Closed

Established: 2015

    This small restaurant, owned and operated by the Hernandez-Jimenez family, serves up an interesting variety of family recipes. In visiting with our server Jessica, I learned that her father has been in the restaurant business for 15 years and developed most of the unique menu offerings. Jessica and her mother run the front of the restaurant while their husbands manage the kitchen.

Chilitto Pikin Mexican Restaurant

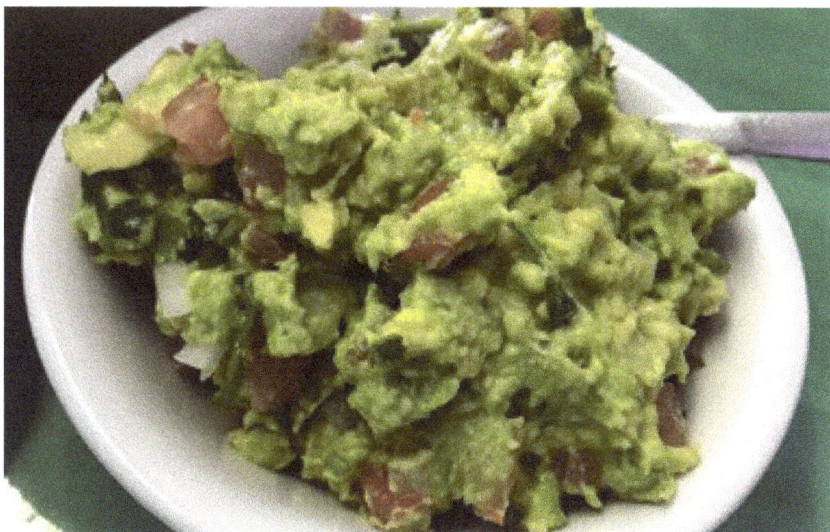

Small Guacamole

Clayton's Beach Bar

"The biggest beach bar in Texas"

6900 Padre Blvd
South Padre Island, TX 78597
956.761.5900

http://claytonsbeachbar.com
Facebook: Claytons Beach Bar and Grill

Open everyday from 11:30 am - 2:00 am

Established: 2011

Patrons enjoy the beach from the huge open deck. Clayton's is known for its special event throughout the year.

Coconuts Bar & Grill

2301 Laguna Drive
South Padre island, TX
956.761.5499
wwwcoconutsspi.com
Facebook: Coconuts SPI

Hours
Sun - Sat 10:00 am - 2:00 am

Bayside dining with a view of SPI's famous sunsets. In addition to the bar and grill, Coconuts also offers parasailing as well as jet-ski and kayak rentals.

Daddy's Cajun Kitchen

1808 Padre Blvd
South Padre Island, TX
956-761-1975

Facebook: Daddy's Seafood & Cajun Kitchen

Open everyday 11:00 am - 10:00 pm

Yes you can experience Cajun food in south Texas. Daddy's offers fresh local seafood dished up Cajun style. You can order dishes such as a seafood botany, Cajun mixup, crawfish étouffée or red bean and rice.

Daddy's is open seven days a week for lunch and dinner and features a full bar. Dirty Al's

Daddy's Cajun Kitchen

Shrimp and Fish Platter with Roasted Red Potatoes

Dirty Al's

33396 State Park Rd
South Padre Island, TX
956-761-4901

www.dirtyalspi.com

Open daily 11:00 am - 8:00 pm

Established: 1986

Alfonso Salazar, better known as "Dirty Al" originally started shrimping as a young man with his father and six brothers. In 2003, he and his youngest son, Cameron, who graduated from Culinary School, transformed his bait stand into a restaurant where together they have been known for having "The World's Best Fried Shrimp"! In 2005, his other two sons returned home to help grow the business.

(Taken from www.dirtyalspi.com)

The Salazar family restaurants include Dirty Al's, Daddy's Cajun Kitchen, Señor Donkey and Liam's Steakhouse in South Padre Island, and Pelican Station in Port Isabel. Dirty Al's also has locations in Brownsville and McAllen.

D' Pizza Joint

2413 Padre Blvd
South Padre Island, TX
956-761-7995

Facebook: D' Pizza Joint

Hours
Mon - Thu 11:00 - 11:00
Fri - Sun 11:00 - 12:00 am

This family-owned restaurant opened on the island in 1983. Pizza is their specialty but they also serve spaghetti, other Italian dishes and American food. Diners can enjoy live music on selected evenings.

Pizza delivery available on the island.

El Papa's Restaurant

814 Garcia
Port Isabel, TX
956-943-7133

Facebook: https://www.facebook.com/pg/ElPapas956/

Hours
Mon 7:30 am - 3:00 pm
Tue 7:30 am - 3:00 pm
Wed 7:30 am - 8:00 pm
Thu 7:30 am - 3:00 pm
Fri 7:30 am - 8:00 pm
Sat 7:30 am - 2:00 pm
Sun Closed

Gabriella's Italian Grill and Pizzeria

700 Padre Blvd
South Padre Island, TX
956.761.6111
Website: www.gabriellasspi.com

2015 & 2016 Certificates of Excellence by TripAdvisor

Hours

Sun - Thu 4:00 pm - 10:00 pm
Fri - Sat 4:00 pm - 11:00 pm

Owners Arnie Creinin and Rick Masso take pride in delivering quality Italian food in South Padre Island. With a passion for all things Italian, they serve specialty items and twelve specialty pizzas. They have the only Italian brick oven in South Texas.

Along with quality, ambiance is king. Gabriella's offers a large wine list and set the mood with the music of greats like Frank Sinatra, Dean Martin and Louis Armstrong. Guests can enjoy indoor or patio seating as well as carryout or delivery.

The Hilton Garden Grill & Bar

7010 Padre Blvd
South Padre Island, TX
956-434-0853

Facebook: The Garden Grille & Bar South Padre Island

Open for Breakfast, Lunch and Dinner 6:00 am - 10:00 pm

American Restaurant

The Garden Grille features a breakfast buffet, lunch and dinner
specials and a full bar with 12 beers on tap.

Grapevine Cafe and Coffee Shop

101 E. Swordfish
South Padre Island, TX
956-761-8463

FB: The Grapevine Cafe & Coffeehouse

Hours:
The - Tue 7:00 am - 3:00 pm
Closed Wednesday

Serving Breakfast and Lunch

JAX

JAX Burgers Fries & Shakes
1912 Padre Blvd
South Padre Island, TX
956-772-8182

www.jaxburgers.com

Monday - Saturday 11am-8pm
Sunday: Closed

JAX Burgers Fries & Shakes first opened in Spring Texas, in 2010. The family-owned-and-operated burger joint prides itself on their 100% fresh angus beef burgers and friendly customer service.

JAX

Burger and fries big enough to split

Joe's Oyster Bar

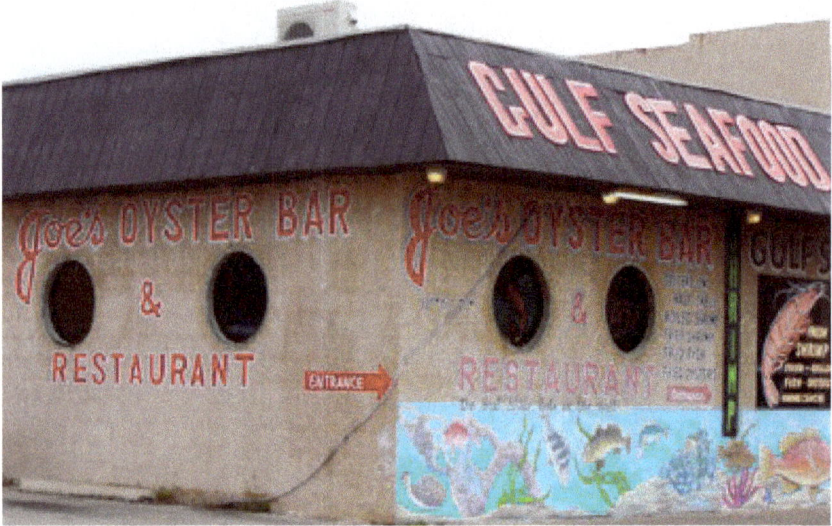

207 Maxan
Port Isabel, TX 78578
956.943.4501

Facebook: Joe's Oyster Bar

(Awarded Tripadvisor.com's 2013 Certificate of Excellence)

Hours:
Sun - Sat 11:00 am - 7:00 pm

Since its opening in the early 1980's, Joe's has been a staple in Port Isabel. Located on Maxan Street, just a couple of blocks west of lighthouse square, Joe's has recently expanded to offer more seating.

Joe's is known for its fresh seafood, offering both a lunch and dinner menu. Patrons enter the restaurant through the seafood market. The restaurant is casual, serving food on paper plates and plastic silverware. As their name implies, they are known for their oysters. Check out online sources like Yelp and TripAdvisor for multiple reviews.

Johnny Rockets

410 Padre Blvd, Ste 108
South Padre Island, TX
956-433-5504

Facebook: Johnny RocketsSPI

Hours:

Sun - Thurs 11:00 am - 10:00 pm
Fri - Sat 11:00 am - 11:00 pm

Hamburger chain that opened in South Padre Island in 2016.

Kelly's Irish Pub

101 E. Morningside Dr.
South Padre Island, TX
956-433-5380

Facebook: Kelly's Irish Pub

Hours:
Sun - Sat 11:00 am - 2:00 am

South Padre's Irish Pub. Great draft beer selection, Irish cuisine, darts, and billiards. Kelly's is a favorite for locals.

Kohnami Sushi Bar and Japanese Steakhouse

410 Padre Blvd
South Padre Island, TX
956-761-2446

www.facebook.com/Kohnami

Laguna Bob's

2401 Laguna Blvd
South Padre island, TX
956-433-5499

www.lagunabob.com

Facebook: Laguna BOB

Open daily at 11:00 am
Known for their seafood, cocktails and sunset views.

Liam's Steak House & Oyster Bar

3409 Padre Blvd
South Padre Island, TX
956-772-4700

http://www.liamssteakhouse.com
Facebook: Liams Steak House

Hours
Sun - Thu 5:00 pm - 10:00 pm
Fri - Sat 5:00 pm - 11:00 pm

Fine dining arrived with the 2013 opening of Liam's Steak House. It is the perfect special-occasion place with its menu of quality steaks, fresh seafood and fine wines.

Liam's was designed by "Dirty" Al Salazar's two sons, Cameron and Ethan.

Los Cabos Mexican Restaurant

309 Port Rd
Port Isabel, TX
956-943-3777

Facebook: Los Cabos
Open everyday 7:00 am - 7:00 pm

Louie's Back yard

2305 Laguna Blvd
South Padre Island, TX
956-761-6406

www.louiesbackyardspi.com
Facebook: Louie's Backyard

Known for their seafood, bar, music and sunset views
All-you-can-eat Prime Rib and Seafood Buffet
Features a full restaurant, upstairs sports bar and live music

Open at 11:30 am daily

Manuel's Mexican Restaurant

313 E. Maxan
Port Isabel, TX 78578
956.943.1655

Facebook: Manuel's Restaurant Port Isabel, Texas

Hours
Tue - Sun 7:00 am - 2:00 pm
Mon Closed

In 1983, Joe and his mother Francesca opened Manuel's in the Padre South Hotel on South Padre Island and began developing menu items that are still favorites today. In 1989, they moved to the location that is currently the Grapevine Cafe and Coffeehouse. After 10 years in that location, they moved their business to Port Isabel, where they've continued as one of the most popular restaurants in the area. Ask reviewers from publications like Rolling Stone, Texas Highways and Texas Monthly, who have all succumbed to the taste of the food and the quality of the service. Although Francesca no longer works in the restaurant, her son, grandsons and a great-grandson carry on her legacy of great food.

Manuel's Mexican Restaurant

1/2 half of a
Chicken Fajita con Todo Enchilada Wrap

Marcello's Italian Restaurant

110 North Tarnava
(On Lighthouse Square)
Port Isabel, TX 78578
956-943-7611

http://wwwmarcellosspi.com
Facebook: Marcello's Italian Restaurant & Bar on the Piazza

Hours
Sun - Sat 11:00 am - 10:00 pm

Now owned and operated by the Friedmans (who also own Pirate's Landing, Pier 19 and Sea Ranch), the Marcello's building has a history dating back to the early 1950s.

Named Lighthouse Grocery, the business was owned by Vincente Gonzales. In 1988, Manuela Stevenson became the owner. She enhanced the building with extensive renovations and opened as Marcello's Italian Restaurant. To this day, it maintains its Mediterranean decor and offers patrons delicious food, good service and an Italian ambiance.

The Meatball Cafe

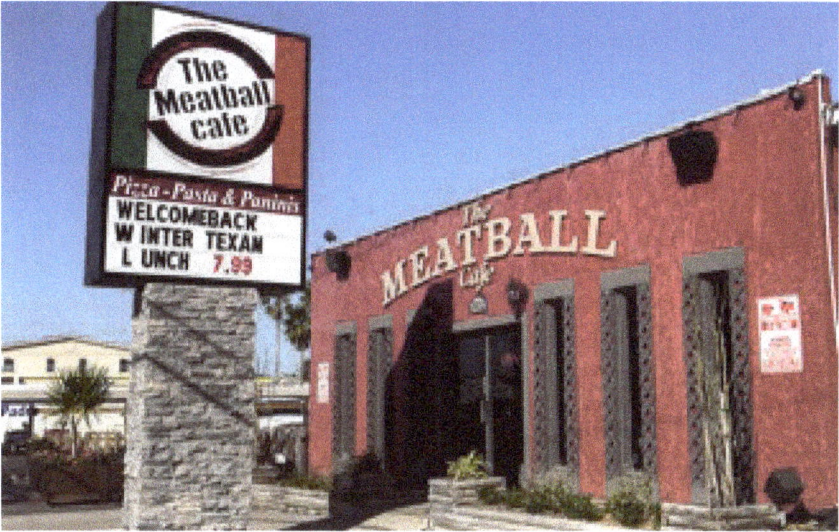

2412 Padre Blvd
South Padre Island, TX
956-299-4605

www.themeatball-cafe.com
Facebook: Meatball Cafe

Hours:
Sun - Thu 11:00 - 9:00
Fri - Sat 11:00 - 10:00

Homemade pasta and sauces with full bar.
Outside dog-friendly patio dining.
Founded in 2015 by Rhonda and John Ferrone, who also own and operate the Southern Wave catamaran sunset dinner cruises.

Padre Island Brewing Company & Restaurant

3400 Padre Blvd
South Padre Island, TX
956-761-9585

http://pibrewingcompany.com/
Facebook: Padre Island Brewing Company

Open 7 days a week at 11:30 am

Established: 1995

Featuring fried shrimp and fish, burgers and a variety of sandwiches. Craft beers fresh brewed on site.

PadreRita Grill

4001 Padre Blvd
South Padre Island, TX
956-761-7482

www.padreritagrillmenufy.com

Hours:
Mon - Thu 11:00 am - 11:30 pm
Fri 11:00 am Midnight
Sat 9:00 am - 2:00 am
Sun 9:00 am - 2:00 am

\Seafood, Steaks, Burgers, Drinks and Music
Daily Specials
Live music: 6:00 - 9:00pm daily
Friday - Saturday Nights Prime Rib, Seafood, Paella and Pasta
Buffet

The Painted Marlin Grille

202 W Whiting
South Padre Island, TX
956-761-2977

www.paintedmarlingrille.com
Facebook: Painted Marlin Grille

Established: 2016

New to the island, the Painted Marlin Grille offers a great place to view sunsets, watch pelicans or simply relax and enjoy food and drink on the bay. It has already become a favorite. I've only been there for happy hour and have loved the margaritas and the sunsets.

Palm Street Pier Bar and Grill

204 Palm Street
South Padre Island, TX
956-772-7256

www.palmstreetpier.com

On the bay, featuring burgers, bar and music

Parrot Eyes Restaurant and Bar

5801 Padre Blvd
South Padre Island, TX
956-772-9040

www.parroteyesspi.com

Hours 11:00 am to 1 hour after sunset
Bayside dining

Pelican's Station
Aka Dirty Al's at Pelican Station

201 S Garcia St
Port Isabel, TX 78578
956.943.3344

FB: Dirty Al's at Pelican Station

Hours
Sun - Thu 7:00 am - 9:00 pm
Fri - Sat 7:00 am - 10:00 pm

Offering Cajun and seafood specialties indoors or on the bayside deck

Pelican Station is located where the Rio Grande Rail Road ran in the late 1800s. RGRR began as the only railroad in Texas and one of the few in the United States. It was a 42" gauge railroad. Consisting of three locomotives and fifty-six cars, it ran a twenty-six mile route between Point Isabel and Brownsville.

Several Brownsville businessmen created the RGRR in an attempt to break the transportation monopoly held by riverboat owners Richard King and Mifflin Kennedy, who later became owners of large ranches in the area.

RGRR had a 1000 foot pier built over the shallow waters of Laguna Madre. Lighter boats ferried cargo to and from the pier from larger ships anchored at sea. This pier was rebuilt in 1928 by the US Corps of Engineers and used to deliver the granite rock used to construct the Jetties.

Pelican Station honors its history with photos, mementos and a railroad track complete with a caboose. Alfonso Salazar (Dirty Al's) and his family own and operate six restaurants on beautiful South Padre Island and Port Isabel.

41

Pier 19 Restaurant & Bar

1 Padre Blvd
South Padre Island, TX
956-761-7437

www.pier19.us or www.pier19southpadre.com

South of the causeway behind the KOA Campground

Open daily at 7:00 am

Serving breakfast, lunch and dinner

Dine on the water on the pier or stroll the boardwalk.
Great view for fun and photography.

Pirate's Landing

110 North Garcia Street
Port Isabel, TX 78578
956- 943-3663

www.pirateslandingportisabel.com

Hours
Everyday 11:00 am - 10:00 pm

Pirate's Landing is located at the original "Point" of the Laguna Madre with a 30-foot bluff where the Port Isabel Lighthouse now stands. The point's strategic location was instrumental to the settlement of Point Isabel and early maritime industry.

The Coahilitecan Indians originally inhabited this land. In the 1500s, Spain sent explorers, but it wasn't until the mid-1700s that Spain awarded land grants to colonists. Doña Rosa Maria Hinojosa inherited the Santa Isabella Land Grant on the Texas Coast. Her son, Padre Nicholas Balli, later obtained the grant to what is now Padre Island.

The Texas coast gained importance to Mexico, the U.S., and smugglers from both countries in the 1800s. Local ranchers formed alliances with pirates who sailed their contraband between the Rio Grande and Corpus Christi. In the 1830s, Don Rafael Garcia established El Fronton de Santa Isabel (Point Isabel) to become the base for the growing Port of Matamoros and the privateer fleet.

In 1846, Fort Polk was established as a supply unit for the U.S. / Mexican War. Many notable men, including Zachary Taylor, Ulysses S. Grant, and Robert E. Lee, were stationed here. In 1952, the Point Isabel Lighthouse was built to serve the maritime industry. It survived the Civil War and numerous hurricanes, becoming Texas' smallest state park in 1952.

(Taken from www.pirateslandingportisabel.com)

Porky's Pit BBQ

318 Queen Isabella Blvd
Port Isabel, TX
956-772-8143

Facebook: porkyspitspi

Open 11:00 am - 8:00 pm daily except Sunday

Red Mango

1800 Padre Blvd, Suite B
South Padre Island, TX
956-299-4921

www.redmangousa.com
www.facebook.com/redmango

Hours:
Sun – Thu 9:00am – 9:00pm
Fri – Sat 9:00am – 10:00pm

Opened 2017

Red Mango serves frozen yogurt that is all-natural, nonfat and lowfat, gluten-free and packed with beneficial live and active probiotic cultures. They are the first frozen yogurt retailer to earn the National Yogurt Association's Live and Active Cultures seal for meeting the required criteria for healthy frozen yogurt. Red Mango recently expanded its menu to include satisfying meal options such as its all-natural made-to-order fruit and yogurt parfaits and fresh fruit smoothies, and also introduced the world's first all-natural probiotic iced teas that are hand-shaken to order. They also serve sandwiches.

Russo's New York Pizzeria

410 Padre Blvd, Ste 101
South Padre Blvd, TX
956-299-4987

Facebook: RussosSPI

Established: 2016

The Russo family opened Russo's in Texas in 1978. Anthony Russo's parents immigrated to the US in 1962. Anthony opened his first Italian restaurant in Clear Lake, TX, in the early 1990's. He wanted to introduce Texas to New York-style pizza. He has since franchised his operation and has more than 30 locations.

Sea Ranch Restaurant & Bar

I Padre Blvd
South Padre Island, TX
956-761-1314

www.searanchrestaurant.com
Facebook: Sea Ranch Restaurant

Hours:
4:30 pm - 10:00 pm Daily

Featuring fresh seafood from the Gulf of Mexico for 35 years.

Senor Donkey Mexican Restaurant

4215 Padre Blvd
South Padre Island, TX
956-761-4843

http://www.thebigdonkey.com
Facebook: Senor Donkey

Hours
Sun - Thu 11:00 - 10:00
Fri - Sat 11:00 - 11:00

Owned by the Alfonso Salazar family of "Dirty Al's" fame, Señor Donkey gives islanders and visitors a taste of authentic Mexican cuisine. Their varied menu includes shrimp enchiladas, fajitas, taquitos al pastor and more. Happy Hour (Monday through Friday, 3:00pm - 6:00pm) treats customers to $3 margaritas and $2 draft beers. Check the sign out front for their daily specials.

Senor Donkey Mexican Restaurant

Senor Donkey's Margarita

Smokey Tails

105 E Amberjack St
South Padre Island, Texas 78597
956-772-8090

www.smokeytailsbbq.com

Hours:
Tues – Wed: 11:00am - 9:00pm
Thu – Sat: 11:00am – 10:00pm
Closed Sundays and Mondays

Full bar
Outdoor dog-friendly patio
Live music as scheduled

Opened in 2015

Smokey Tails BBQ is a family-owned restaurant serving Kansas City Style barbecue. The restaurant offers a wide variety of menu items. Add fresh seafood and steaks to the standard barbecue fare, and Smokey Tails provides an all-around dining experience for the whole family. The restaurant also has TVs for the sports-minded, a patio for outdoor dining and live entertainment, and a full service bar.

Smokey Tails

BBQ Brisket

Ted's Restaurant

5717 Padre Blvd
South Padre Island, TX
956-761-5327

Facebook: Ted's Restaurant

Hours
Everyday 7:00 - 2:00

In South Padre Island, Ted's and pecan pancakes are practically synonymous. A favorite breakfast and brunch spot for locals and visitors.

Ted Kennett and his sister Karen built and opened Ted's in 1978. After four years, Ted left South Padre Island and Karen has operated the restaurant ever since. She loves the island, her business and her customers. She takes pride in her long-term employees who have become friends. In her own words, she is "happy as a clam.

Ted's is open for breakfast and lunch seven days a week. The restaurant seats 70 and is frequently filled to capacity.

Ted's Restaurant

Ted's famous pecan pancakes

Tequila Sunset Restaurant & Bar

200 Pike Street
South Padre Island, TX
956-761-6198

Bayside restaurant with open air bar.

Open 24 hours every day.
Offering live music and beautiful sunsets.
Free wifi.

Tom & Jerry's Beach Club Bar & Grill

"Home of the Indoor Beach Party"

3212 Padre Blvd
South Padre Island, TX
956-761-8999

Facebook: Tom & Jerry's Beach Club Bar and Grill

Open daily 11:00 am - 11:00 pm

Opened in the Rio Grande Valley in 1977 and expanded to the island in 1996.

Sports bar and BUZZTIME NTN Trivia.

Wanna Wanna Inn Beach Bar & Grill

5100 Gulf Blvd (at Beach Access 19)
South Padre Islandm TX
956-761-7677

Facebook: Wanna Wanna SPI

Opens at 11:30am. Closing time varies with seasons.
Located at the pet-friendly Wanna Wanna Inn.

White Sands Restaurant

418 TX-100
(Located next door to the White Sands Motel)
Port Isabel, TX
956-943-2414

www.facebook.com/whitesandstexas

Serving Breakfast, Lunch and Dinner
Offering American, Mexican and Seafood dishes.

Open Tues - Sun 7:00 am - 7:00 pm

On the Port Isabel Channel with good sunset views

Will & Jack's Burger Shack and Beer Garden

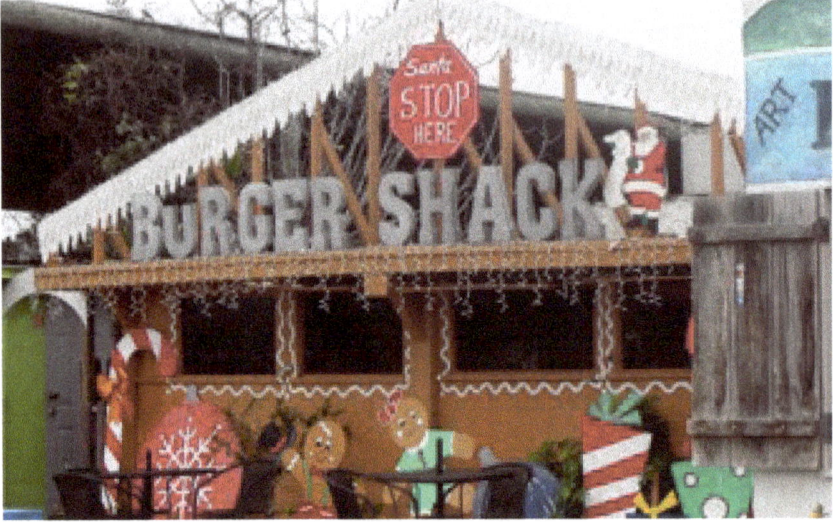

413 E Maxan St.
Port Isabel, TX 78578
956.640.7440

http://www.willandjacksburgershack.com
Facebook: Will and Jacks Burger Shack & Beer Garden

Open
Sun - Thu 11:00 am - 8:00 pm
Fri - Sat 11:00 am - 10:00 pm

Will & Jack's is famous for their burgers, Lola's Most Wanted Nachos and the beer garden. It's a great place to sit outside - either in their beer garden or out in front - and enjoy the beautiful south Texas weather.

Order your burger by number and enjoy options such as #1, the Gigi Burger, topped with artichoke hearts, crispy bacon and melted provolone cheese. Or maybe you'd prefer #11, the Greek Style Lamb Burger, with tzatziki sauce.

Yummies Bistro

700 Padre Blvd, Unit J
South Padre Island, TX

956-761-2526
Facebook: Yummies Bistro

Open Everyday 8:00 am - 2:00 pm

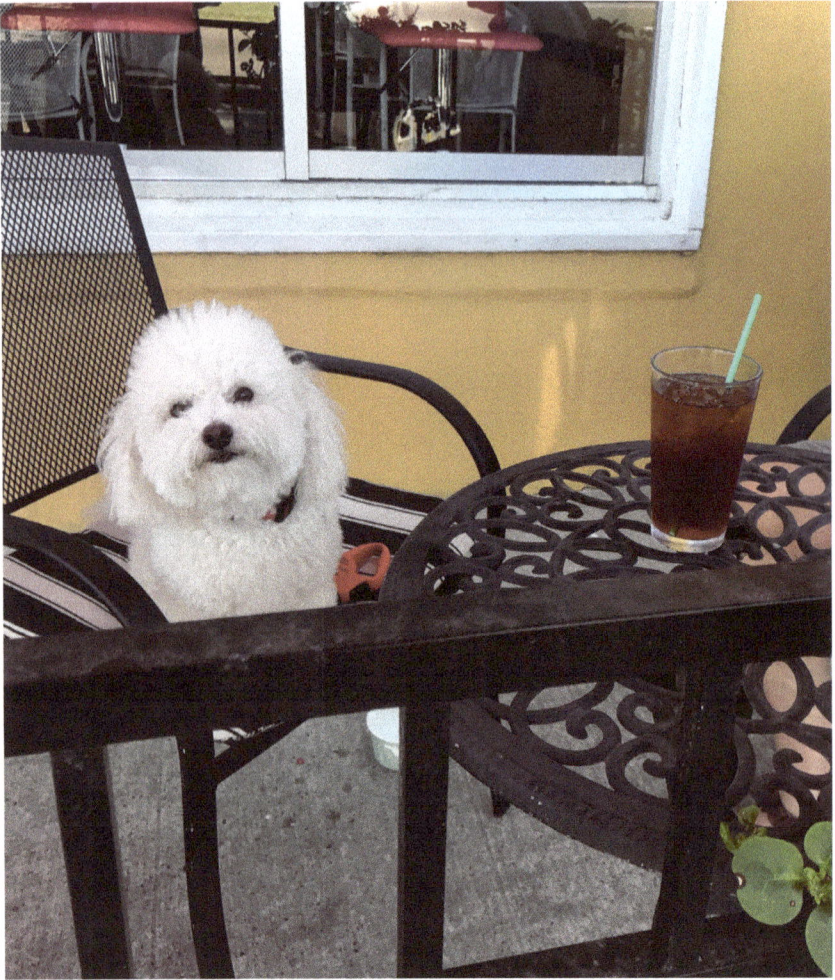

Luke enjoying Causeway Cafe

Dog-friendly locations

(On patio dining. Dogs leashed.)

Port Isabel

Causeway Cafe
Will and Jack's Burger Shack

South Padre Island

Boomerang Billy's
BurgerFi
Clayton's
Gabriella's Italian Grill & Pizzeria
Jax Burgers
PadreRitaGrill
Smokey Tails BBQ
Wanna Wanna Beach Bar & Grill
Yummies Bistro

www.ingramcontent.com/pod-product-compliance
Lightning Source LLC
Chambersburg PA
CBHW042102060426

42446CB00046B/3467